D0151497

BEN CUNNINGHAM

A Life with Color

by Cindy Nemser

JPL Art Publishers / Texas

Copyright © 1989 by JPL Art Publishers, Post, Texas. All rights reserved.
No part of this publication may be reproduced or transmitted in any form
or by any means, electronic or mechanical, including photocopying,
recording, or any information storage and retrieval system, without per-
mission in writing from the publisher.

Library of Congress Cataloging in Publication Data: **88-83969**

ISBN   09622235-0-6

Printed in Hong Kong by South China Printing Co. (1988) Limited

Published by JPL Art Publishers, Post, Texas.

Production Consultant: William Rose
Cover/jacket: MRP Design

Master of color theory, Ben Cunningham used an intricate structure to formulate his passionate response to visual stimuli. His work combined logic with imagination to add new dimensions to our experience of color. In a period of radical change in the cultural environment and of social confrontation and protest, he reaffirmed the underlying principles of perception that unite humanity. As the critic Lawrence Campbell has observed, he was "in the tradition of the masters of pictorial illusion who sought answers in science to the problems they set for themselves in art and who produced results as irreversible as the invention of photography and the vacuum tube."[1]

Ben Cunningham was born on February 10, 1904, in Cripple Creek, Colorado, to Benjamin Frazier Cunningham, Sr., a Boston physician of Scottish origin (who had moved to the western mountain region for reasons of health), and his Canadian-born wife, Clara Shaw, also of Scottish ancestry. The youngest of three brothers, Ben was two and a half years old when the family moved further west to the then small town of Reno, Nevada, 4000 feet above sea level on the eastern side of the Sierra Nevada mountains. This environment affected him intensely. Later he would say, "To grow up in the dry, open desert country with unlimited space and the glorious illumination and excitement—I suppose that is a fortuitous event that would make a visual voluptuary of me at the age of eight."[2] Indeed, all his work reflects the crisp definition and clarity of the desert landscape.

While its setting may have been inspirational, the newly settled and isolated town of Cunningham's youth, with its transient population of miners, ranch hands, and railroad men, was hardly a sympathetic environment for a professional career in the arts. Nor was there any tradition of the visual arts in his family. His father, however, was musical and had organized a little band in Boston while taking his medical degree. Later on, Cunningham also became involved in music, playing jazz trumpet, but for father and son, music remained an avocation.

Thus, little art and few artifacts existed to stimulate the visual imagination of a child growing up in the Reno of those years. Cunningham remembered being taken as a small boy to see a painting in a department store Christmas display. What he saw was probably a sentimental genre scene but to him it was a magical and overwhelming experience. He went on to draw a great deal during his high school years and illustrated the yearbook, but no one ever suggested that he become an artist.

Photographs of Ben Cunningham during those early years suggest an idyllic childhood. He was the protected youngest child of a prominent local family. The whole desert was his playground. He collected Indian arrowheads and rode his own horse to school. But when Cunningham was 13 his seemingly secure world collapsed. His father went off as a medical officer to serve in World War I, fell in love with a woman doctor, and never returned home. Later, Cunningham sought out his father and established a close rapport, but the event left a permanent emotional scar.

Existence became a struggle for the Cunningham family, although Cunningham's maternal uncle, David LeBaron Shaw, also a doctor, came to their aid. In spite of family hopes that he study medicine, Cunningham ultimately enrolled in a pre-architectural course at the University of Nevada but found the studies uninteresting. He dropped out and spent several years wandering around Nevada and California working at odd jobs.

At the time, liberal Nevada divorce laws were attracting a new element to Reno. International socialites, moneyed people from the east, and cultivated Europeans were rubbing elbows with local ranchers, cowboys, miners, and gamblers. Whenever back in Reno, Cunningham was much in demand as an escort for unattached divorcees at local parties. Both his close boyhood friend, Arthur Lyon, and the artist Reuben Kadish, who knew him later in San Francisco and then in New York, have testified that Cunningham was always attractive to women. A photograph taken around 1926 shows him as a tall, handsome, young man of athletic build with an engaging smile. It may have been at the home of Judge George Bartlett, as famous for his parties as for his divorce adjudications, that Cunningham met Juliette Wheeler. Several years his senior, she was attractive, French-born, and married to a wealthy San Francisco business man. Arthur Lyon has suggested that she was the object of Cunningham's first real emotional involvement, but, more significantly, she introduced Cunningham to the European attitude that art was a serious and respected profession. Their affair, if there was one, may have been brief, but her influence on his life was profound and permanent. It was Juliette Wheeler who recognized Cunningham's fervor for the visual arts and encouraged him to study painting in San Francisco.

In later years, he remembered wrapping his paint box in newspaper to avoid being identified as an artist, and walking around the block several times before finding the courage to enroll in an art school. "When I said I wanted to register," he reminisced, "I waited for a bolt from heaven to strike me. All they said was 'Fine, pay your tuition.' "[3]

Cunningham home under construction, 441 Cheney Street, Reno, 1910

Dr. and Mrs. Benjamin Cunningham, Sr. with three sons (left to right): Jack, Ben, Fred

Ben Cunningham,
1915

Ben on horseback, 1917

Ben Cunningham near Reno, 1929

Cunningham at easel, Reno, c. 1929

Cunningham began his studies at the Mark Hopkins Art Institute (later called the California School of Fine Arts, and, today, the San Francisco Art Institute) in 1925 and took courses there intermittently for the next three years. Always financially pressed, he worked at odd jobs in San Francisco and in Reno to pay for tuition and materials.

At the school, he studied every aspect of the visual arts, including drawing, painting and sculpture. A gifted student, he easily mastered drawing, as can be seen by his accomplished realistic self-portrait done later in 1935. However, because drawing came so easily, he soon lost interest in it. This distaste for the facile lasted all his life, and later he would warn his own students not to let skill get ahead of imagination. Ray Boynton was the painting teacher he most admired and by whom he was most influenced. They often went together to Contra Costa county across San Francisco Bay to do sketches and pastels of the hills, rounded and voluptuous in comparison to the skeletal mountains of Nevada. Cunningham resisted advice from other instructors to "loosen up," rejecting the notion that highly structured painting was in any way antipathetic to feeling. He would encounter the same prejudice much later during the heyday of Abstract Expressionism, but always he would see form as a means of expression rather than as a constraint.

Color was Cunningham's particular focus in his studies. He had seen, during his formative years in the monochromatic landscape of bare mountains and sagebrush, that light and shadow affected color dramatically. Instinctively, he knew it was light not drawing that translated into color, but as yet he had no rigorous system with which to work out the correct translations. Here his teachers had little knowledge to offer him. They taught him the Munsell System to help him mix color pigments, but then assured him, "There's nothing to learn. Being a colorist is a gift." Cunningham felt frustrated. He wanted to understand more about color relationships and why certain interactions occurred.

Cunningham left school permanently around 1929. The next few years were a time of continued financial struggle. During much of 1929 and 1930 he was in Reno, working as a purchasing agent for a mining company, but returned to San Francisco late in 1930, settling into a small studio. In 1931, he produced his first major work, NUDE WITH PINK RIBBON, which he showed in a small co-op gallery. The painting, its central figure modeled more with light than with line, is a precursor of work to come. It was influenced by a reproduction of a Titian VENUS which Cunningham saw in a store window every day en route to his studio and unconsciously transferred compositionally to his painting. Only afterward did Cunningham realize what had happened, and for the rest of his professional life, always tried to keep direct influences of other artists out of his work. In this painting, his intense sense of design is already evident in the repeated patterns of the coverlet, in the lines of the body that reiterate the curves of the cushion, in the sweep

Self-Portrait. 1935. Tempera on wood, 15 × 12″. Collection, Patsy Cunningham.

Nude with Pink Ribbon. 1931. Oil on canvas, 18 × 26″. Collection, Patsy Cunningham.

of the young man's arms and in the folds of the California hills. There is an ordered progression of color from sky to water to window to the deeper green of the curtain. When the painting was hung in a group show, it created a stir that won Cunningham a one-man exhibition the following year. That show marked the beginning of his acceptance into the circles that made up the San Francisco art scene, but despite positive critical reviews, he received no significant financial support, a common experience of artists there at that time.

In 1931, Cunningham married the gifted artist Marion Osborn, whose talent in the silk-screen medium, combined with a practical grasp of financial matters, created a growing market for her charming prints of San Francisco scenes. During the next few years, still searching and experimenting, Cunningham himself found no solution to economic survival through his work, although in 1934 he was one of the artists commissioned by the Public Works of Art Project to paint murals in San Francisco's Coit Tower. An easel painting of 1936, WOMAN WITH A MIRROR, continued to define the figure with light but also showed the influence of Persian painting in its flat, patterned aspects.

Marion Osborn Cunningham, c. 1933

Woman with a Mirror. 1936. Oil on canvas board, 22½ × 15½".
Collection, Clotildes Gleiberman, New York City. Photo: Otto Nelson.

That year Cunningham went to work for the Federal Art Project on a regular basis. His conciliatory temperament made him an ideal administrator, and he became supervisor of mural painting for the Northern California area. After a year, however, he found that he longed to work as an artist—and began to do so at a considerable reduction in pay. During the next two years he completed a number of works in various media including a mural, RESOURCES OF THE SOIL, for the Ukiah Post Office. He took great satisfaction in these projects and many years later reminisced:

> *Working for the Federal Art Project in San Francisco was in most ways a stimulating and rewarding experience. In many of the projects several artists worked as teams, which brought the stimulation of joint enterprise instead of the ivory tower of "self expression." Artists were turned loose to do a total environment which might incorporate such diverse elements as photomurals, weaving, architectural embellishments.*

> *The whole activity was one which the artist himself controlled. . . . . In retrospect, the feeling then was that art was something to experience directly, for excitement and satisfaction, rather than to evaluate in terms of the latest verbal label and fashion. There was a sense of constancy and progression rather than a new sensation every season. The incorporation of art into architecture gave it added meaning in terms of time. Earnings, though slight, freed the artist from debilitating financial anxiety.*[4]

Resources of the Soil. 1939. Tempera on canvas, 5'10" × 12'. Courtesy of the U.S. Postal Service.

Although the '30s were a time of stress for Cunningham both financially and personally (his marriage ended in 1937), it was also a breakthrough decade for him as a painter. During that period, the artist Hilaire Hiler came to San Franciso fresh from Paris where he had been moving in a direction Cunningham had been seeking for years, namely, the development of a formal color system based on the Ostwald color structure. In Hiler, Cunningham found for the first time a person with whom he could discuss color in a knowledgeable manner.

Hiler's concept of structuralism was an attempt to make a genuine connection between science and art. He had discovered that "color, freed from the necessity of being representational, took on a new importance and placed the artist face to face with a new series of responsibilities which perhaps wait to be solved."[5]

Vincent Schmidt, author of "The Structuralism of Hiler and Its Relationship to Other Tendencies in Art," observes:

> *Color to Hiler is basic to painting and, in its structuring, he carries on the work begun by Newton, down through Ridgeway and Ostwald, and paints pictures in which there are as many as four thousand related shades and tones. A structuralist painting is executed in terms of color not in terms of pigments. Hiler considers pigments merely as a collection of coloring materials with purely fortuitous or hit-and-miss relations which do not mean color any more than noise means music. Before color relations are of interest an orderly arrangement must be made.*[6]

Hiler also insisted that "by the utilization of the scientific method, the contemporary artist will be enabled to create for himself a new instrument."[7] He declared further that "this use of the intellect need no more stifle the intelligence of the heart or the capacity for feeling on the part of the painter than the knowledge of harmony, counterpoint, and the rules of musical composition stifle that of the composer in possession of a well-tuned piano."[8]

Hiler's ideas had a profound influence on Cunningham's thinking, and he felt particularly indebted to the older artist for introducing him to the Ostwald Color System.

Cunningham saw that the Ostwald System created a credible theory for the threshold of perception and stressed color perceived "psychologically" rather than as specific mixtures of paint. The Ostwald System adjusts every color the human mind can distinguish (actually many more than most people can visualize) in its proper relation to every other color. Cunningham expressed his gratitude for Ostwald's contribution when he wrote, "The chemist Wilhelm Ostwald's structuralization of color was, for me, a map which opened up a new territory for visual exploration."[9]

Cunningham ultimately modified Ostwald's ideas and explained to Faber Birren, distinguished author of many books on color, that he had substituted the terms "materialized" and "dematerialized" for Ostwald's "related" and "unrelated" color. "Related" refers to the black content common to all color in pigment; in this sense, the color in light is "unrelated." Thus, when Cunningham would speak of dematerialized color as a goal he meant he was trying to achieve the illusion of removing black content from pigment and transforming it into light.[10]

Explaining the difference between himself and some other painters the artist stated:

> *Some think of pigments as color, confusing the stimulus with the response. Pigment is a tool; response is comprehension. One can be a good colorist with black, white, and gray only. It's the dematerialization of the materials (pigments) which is important to me.*[11]

Like his mentor Hiler, Cunningham used exact methods in his color work, but never equated scientific explorations or exactitudes with the art he produced. He made clear his belief that "the meaning of painting is always greater than the man and his tools."[12] He also stressed that painting is a continuous exploration of our visual universe—an attempt to find the structure and order behind the appearance of things, not merely to look but to *see*. He went on to underline that in this search he regarded the eye and the imagination as inseparable and emphasized the fact that in the act of seeing, the image occurs not on the retina but in the visual cortex, and to interpret it we draw on our total experience and memory bank. The painter's objective, he felt, is to enrich this experience by inventing new ways of seeing.[13]

Faber Birren's carefully annotated books on color led Cunningham to other rich source material: Chevreul, Helmholtz, and books on neo-impressionism. He was particularly influenced by David Katz's *World of Color*, written in 1911 and translated from the German in 1937. Katz defined the three essential ways in which we experience color, namely, as surface, film, or volume.[14] Stated simply, one *looks at* a surface color (such as a painted wall), one *looks through* a film color (a shadow or an illumination), and one *looks into* a volume color (for example, the blue of the sky or the depths of a clear lake).

Cunningham's interpretation of art history was that Renaissance painting had dematerialized space and that Cubism had dematerialized form. His goal, he believed, was to dematerialize color, that is, to transform inert pigment into shifting patterns of light and shadow. "Color without illusion is barn paint," was a favorite quotation. To create his illusions he became intensely involved with film color, which lends itself to numerous combinations and permutations, and with it he created some of his most original and memorable images.

This original work came later in his career. For a time after being introduced to the Ostwald Color System, Cunningham painted in a manner similar to Hiler's. The older artist's influence on him can be seen in his painting, MUSICIANS, an essentially Cubist rendition done in 1936. It is a work that directly reflects the period in which he was involved with jazz music. As noted earlier, he played the trumpet, and, during a brief pilgrimage to the Chicago jazz scene, was considered sufficiently accomplished to cut a record with Eddie Condon as a stand-in for one of the group's regulars. The painting also demonstrates an early use of film color seen here as light. He did other versions of this theme in 1939 and in 1940–41, and returned to it in his 1972 painting, JAZZ REMINISCENCE.

Musicians III. 1941. Oil on canvas board, 24 × 20″. Collection, Arthur Lyon, Boise, Idaho. Photo: George Karfiol.

In the spring of 1939, Cunningham finally went to Paris. Mural work for the San Francisco World's Fair of that year financed the trip that had been a long-term goal. The painter responded wholeheartedly to the "city of light" and reveled in seeing great modern paintings he had heretofore known only in reproduction. Among the artists he met was a young, attractive, Norwegian woman with whom he spent some idyllic summer weeks at the Brittany shore. The result of that experience was a painting called AFTERIMAGE OF BRITTANY, which reflects the influence of the school of Paris. The Cunningham vision, however, is to be found in the work's strong sense of design and an early use of additive film color that creates the illusion of light. Characteristic of the artist's future work is the ambiguity of the figure and ground, the pattern of the wall paper, and the graded progression of blue slats with black shadows. There is also an indication of his geometric bent in the use of the basic figure 8 as a shorthand reference to the female form.

When the outbreak of World War II in Europe forced Cunningham's return to San Francisco toward the end of 1939, his life and art were still in an unsettled state. His marriage was over; both his parents had died as the result of separate automobile accidents; his brother Jack was also dead, tragically young; his financial situation remained precarious. Moreover, he had still not found the images that were to be the expressive vehicles for his color explorations. At that time, he did several paintings that were precursors of works to come. There is THE DESERT, with its skull, its threatening blackness, its sense of intense heat and its eerie white light. This is the first time that Cunningham incorporated a frame into a painting and extended film color over it. THE DESERT has an ominous, surreal quality that expresses the destructive forces of nature. This sense of unease occasionally turns up in the artist's later works during stressful periods of his life.

Another desert landscape of the period, PYRAMID LAKE, 1941, presents an interesting stylistic contrast. Possibly because it was done for his dearly loved brother Fred, this painting is more realistically treated than was typical of Cunningham's painting at the time. There is the image of the stark, bare Nevada mountains that resemble elephant hide, the austerity of the monochromatic sagebrush and the sudden vision of the turquoise lake that bursts upon one like a welcome oasis. Here Cunningham became involved in volume color because he could see the almost measurable gradation in color from brown to blue as the mountains receded into the distance. This majestic painting with its severe, stately mountains is related in style to the pastels he did of the yellow California hills during his earlier student days.

Afterimage of Brittany. 1939. Oil on canvas, 20 × 29″. Collection, Patsy Cunningham.

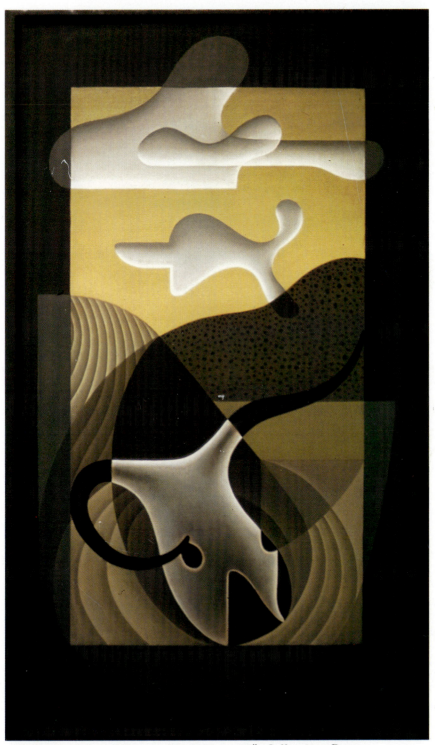

The Desert. 1939. Oil on wood, 48¾ × 29″. Collection, Patsy Cunningham.

Pyramid Lake. 1941. Oil on canvas, 29 × 57″. Collection, Patsy Cunningham.

Metameric Moving Van. 1941. Wax on canvas board, 20 × 26″. Private collection.

METAMERIC MOVING VAN, also painted in 1941, is a good example of how an outside stimulus can trigger an idea for a painting. Cunningham saw a moving van painted many different brilliant hues and became keyed up about this sudden thrust of color on his consciousness. He was delighted with the transformation of an ordinary service vehicle into a conveyance of chromatic splendor. One feels that the artist had fun with this painting, almost hiding the words "moving van" in his abstract design. In order to visualize his idea, he used the concept of metameric color which meant juxtaposing two colors of equal value. The values being equal, it is impossible to focus on either color for long and a shimmering effect is created in the painting. Many artists used this device later on, but Cunningham seldom returned to it in his work.

A second marriage, to Helen Maxwell, took place in 1941, but it, too, did not endure. In December of that year, the United States entered the war and the following month Cunningham went into training as a naval architect. Accomplished at his job, Cunningham worked long hours on blueprints for destroyers and cruisers but still found time to paint in his studio, mostly at night.

In 1942, Cunningham did a painting that reflects this difficult personal period of his life. It was called INCUBUS, meaning nightmare. This work with its disturbingly agitated shapes is his first totally abstract painting and makes use of film color, once again extended into the frame, but handled rather simplistically. Sand is also combined with some pigments to hold certain colors on the surface in contrast with the colors seen through illusionary films.

Above, Cunningham with Nevada friend Arthur Lyon in San Francisco studio, c. 1942

Cunningham with Bertha Lyon, San Francisco, c. 1943

Incubus. 1942. Oil on canvas board, 15 × 21″. Collection, Bertha Lyon, Carson City, Nevada.

It was at this time that Cunningham met Patsy Griffin, a co-worker for the Navy, whom he later married. She was to be his close companion and confidante for over 30 years.

In April of 1944, Patsy moved to New York City and in October, Cunningham arrived there to be with her. He welcomed the move away from San Francisco where he felt there was interest, but little support for art at that time. Bertha Lyon, the wife of his Reno friend Arthur, had been one of his few patrons. As Reuben Kadish has remarked, "With the number of galleries and museums in New York, it was an art community where gambling odds were much higher in the artist's favor than in San Francisco."[15]

The couple occupied a minuscule apartment in Greenwich Village which, according to Patsy, "underlooked" a garden and, for the next few years, struggled to survive financially. Among the odd jobs that came the painter's way were working with a designer on murals for the Polo Room at the Westbury Hotel and teaching drawing at the Jamesine Franklin School on Park Avenue.

Then in 1946, Cunningham obtained a position at the Newark School of Fine & Industrial Arts in New Jersey, and thus began a serious and illustrious teaching career. During his 14-year tenure, he became a strong influence on many students, painter Robert Zakanitch among them. He was instrumental in bringing in other sophisticated colorists as teachers, including Hilaire Hiler and Bauhaus-trained Hannes Beckmann who had been inspired by Cunningham to return to painting and color work. Cunningham himself designed a course called Color Form and, according to Zakanitch:

> He was incredible as a teacher. The information that he knew was so vast it took on another dimension. The system was so impeccably thought out that once you got through Cunningham, everyone else was easy. I read Albers's book. It was ABC. Because of Cunningham's teaching and my understanding of it, I never had any color problems in my art. For me, I owe him this incredible debt. I can't even measure that.[16]

Another student, Frank Gauna, knew Cunningham on a more personal level and wrote of him:

> He was so different than anyone I'd ever met. His manner, his dress, his calm intelligent way of talking and the interest he showed in a student had a civilizing effect on me. He was a friend who was trying to put me on a path that 24 years later led me to a show in Madrid. Never a day goes by that I paint that I don't think of Ben.[17]

26

It was in the late '40s that Cunningham began to find his own mature voice as a painter with a work entitled DUCK ON A GLOVE COUNTER, done in 1947. It grew out of a pencil sketch he did for some friends as a Christmas card. The painting was conceived of as a totally abstract complicated study in film color. Later, the title suggested itself because of the light-hearted shapes resembling fingers, and the duck-like configuration in the lower right-hand corner. The forms seem to move forward and backward continually in a green volume. Color is manipulated freely; later the artist often worked from preliminary color structures.

After moving to New York, Cunningham's paintings became almost totally abstract. Ideas evolved purely from his imagination, although, on occasion, an outside event could still act as a stimulus. Having grown up in the dramatic and vast desert country of the West, he was not inspired aesthetically by the more crowded and confined spaces of New York City and had to create his own visual world.

Duck on a Glove Counter. 1947. Oil on canvas, 30 × 48″. Private collection. Photo: George Karfiol.

In 1948, he began the CORNER PAINTING, his major breakthrough work. The initial idea evolved out of reading David Katz's *World of Color* which, we have already noted, defined the three modes of appearance of color as surface, film, and volume. Katz said these three aspects of color could not exist simultaneously in the same work. Cunningham thought they could, set out to prove it, and in this work succeeded in doing so. In this gold-volumed painting, he mixed sand into the pigment to keep some geometric forms on the surface and made use of both additive (adding light) and subtractive (removing light) films. The painting, designed to fit into a corner, anticipated the shaped canvases of the '60s. This two-paneled work gives the illusion of two planes that intersect and recede into a space that does not exist. Faber Birren later wrote of it:

> As an example of what might be called geometric abstraction or geometric non-objectivism, this work is quite a masterpiece. If it has the look of being done with mirrors give Cunningham credit for the whole original effect. As the viewer gives his attention, he begins to sense dimension and distance. The forms are not on flat surfaces; they are suspended and seem to float stably in space. The colors, mostly in the gold to orange to red range, are dominated by a yellowish illumination; they contribute to the impression of a dream world in which the fantasy of the artist indicates method in madness.[18]

When artist Jean Varda saw the CORNER PAINTING, he wrote to Cunningham, "You speak to God in numbers and those numbers make an ecstatic prayer."[19]

Corner Painting. 1948–50. Oil on 2 canvas panels, 25½ × 36½″, 25½ × 21½″. Collection, Patsy Cunningham.

JOSEPH'S COAT, the second major work undertaken in 1948, was inspired by a tailor's pattern that came under the artist's scrutiny. It consisted of the paper forms used by a tailor to cut out a coat and included the back, sleeves, and pocket. Cunningham moved the pieces around to make a general design of them and then proceeded to do some sophisticated color work. The style of the painting has been influenced by Synthetic Cubism in that the coat is taken apart and the planes overlap. However, some fascinating color games are enacted. On close inspection, one notices that the color that appears to be yellow in the lower left-hand corner is the identical hue to the color that appears green in the upper right. Placing colors in different contexts became a major focus of the artist's work from then on. He often observed that 90% of the neurons in the human nervous system are in the eyes. This scientific fact inspired his stated goals as a painter which were "to organize, to communicate, to delight, to teach new ways of seeing, especially in the realm of color."[20]

Certain patterns and combinations appear in paintings throughout Cunningham's career, and it is interesting to note that the cubes from AFTERIMAGE OF BRITTANY turn up again in JOSEPH'S COAT. This work is an incredibly complex investigation into film color, but unlike the CORNER PAINTING, it does not explore volume color but remains a figure against a white ground.

According to Patsy Cunningham and others who knew him, Cunningham had a sensitivity to color far beyond the average endowment. He could visualize about 700 colors, whereas the ordinary human threshold of color perception is 480 colors, with most people having scarcely any memory for color at all. Just by looking at a color, Cunningham could identify the hue, relate it to every other hue, and analyze its black and white content. It was the equivalent of having perfect pitch in music.

The decade of the '40s ended with a small windfall for the Cunninghams. Payment for the painting NEVADA, commissioned by the Container Corporation of America for their States series, was added to their small savings and made possible a four-month stay in Paris. It was a kind of delayed honeymoon, as they had legalized their union the year before, on May 1, 1948. They rented an apartment on the Left Bank, near the Quai Voltaire, with enough space for the artist to set up a summer studio. The apartment belonged to the actor Albert Rémy and his wife, Yliane, an artist whom Cunningham had known in San Francisco. Rémy spent much of the summer with the Cunninghams, and they in turn visited the Rémy summer home, an old stone farmhouse high on a mountainside above the Rhône Valley. The painting AFTERIMAGE OF NÎMES, with its golden light of the Midi, expresses some of the joy of that summer.

Joseph's Coat. 1950. Oil on canvas board, 24 × 20″. Collection, Peter and Thelma Manjos, La Jolla, California.

Cunningham at easel, Greenwich
Street studio, New York, c. 1948

Ben and Patsy Cunningham, Paris,
1949

At this point, Cunningham's pioneering work in color, dating from the '30s, was still not generally recognized. As someone later wrote, "If a conference had then been held of American painters interested in color theory as applied to painting, it could have been held in a phone booth since only Cunningham and Hiler were involved in it."[21] True, Moholy-Nagy had done a few paintings using films in the '20s which Cunningham might have seen via reproduction, and Albers, Kandinsky, and Klee at the Bauhaus used the Ostwald Color System, but there was no direct contact between these artists and himself.

However, Cunningham's work was beginning to be known in New York and, although he did not have gallery representation, he did sell his work from time to time. In 1950, he was invited to exhibit in a group show at the prestigious Stable gallery. Professionally, though, he still felt quite alone. At one point, Hilaire Hiler appeared briefly in New York to compare notes and paintings with Cunningham, and suggested it was time to make a statement of principles through a group exhibition. But the idea never got off the ground as there were few likely participants in a New York art scene dominated by the Abstract Expressionists. Later in the decade, Cunningham was in the inaugural exhibition at the Collector's Gallery at Yale, along with Joseph Albers, Ellsworth Kelly, and Ad Reinhardt. Much later, in 1971, in Concord, New Hampshire, in a show called *Perception and Illusion: the Marriage of Art and Science* at the Art Center in Hargate, his work appeared with that of Albers, Vasarely, and Anuszkiewicz, artists whose development of optical illusions and color relationships had some connection with his own concerns.

For the most part, however, Cunningham was isolated from any group due to the complexity of his ideas. His student, Robert Zakanitch, analyzed his position in this way: "He was an incredible color mind who never simplified his ideas or latched on to some simple-minded execution like some other artists who were thought of as colorists. It was difficult for people who were used to the simplistic to comprehend what he was up to."[22]

Like many artists, Cunningham had a love-hate relationship with success. He wanted it but feared being corrupted by it. He articulated his feelings by saying, "The outside world cannot be all that important to a painter. If he allows it to be, his inner world suffers."[23] As he put it, " 'Success' to an artist most often means the opportunity to reap rewards for adapting to society's fashion of the moment. True success means recognition of the artist's individual vision and contribution, and that remains elusive."[24]

Yet these statements did not mean that Ben Cunningham cared nothing for his public's response. He thrived on recognition and positive reaction to his work whenever it came, but he winced at the notion of being a careerist or a "maker of merchandise," as he often put it.

In the same vein, whenever he could afford them, Cunningham wore elegant clothes—capes, Norfolk jackets, and British berets—because he enjoyed them. However, although he was conscious of the admiration they elicited from others—the artist Abe Ajay would write later of his friend's "private grace and splendid sartorial style"[25]—he was the most natural of men and would never dress for public consumption.

In any case, as the '40s ended, there were few superstars in the small New York art world, and those that did emerge were in the Abstract Expressionist mode. Indeed, there was, at this time, a definite hostility to any formalistic approach to art.

It was to this atmosphere that Cunningham returned from Paris, refreshed visually and spiritually, late in 1949. The following year the artist did several key works, beginning with TORSION (started in Paris), a painting made up of rectangles that move in opposite directions simultaneously. The brilliant glow of the rectangle closest to the viewer's eye is entrancing as it seems to pour off light from the surface, but then the light diminishes as forms recede into the volume color. The theme of this work preoccupied the painter for years, and he returned to it in 1955, and again in 1965 with TORSION IV, where the rectangles are patterned with squares. (Cunningham often worked on a painting or explored a theme over a period of time). The twisting of the images may have been a visualization of a restless force within him—perhaps a metaphor for art—the struggle to bring forth light, to make a visual statement out of the artist's innate creativity.

Torsion II. 1950. Oil on canvas board, 18¼ × 24¼".
Collection, Góran and Catharina Bauer, Sweden.

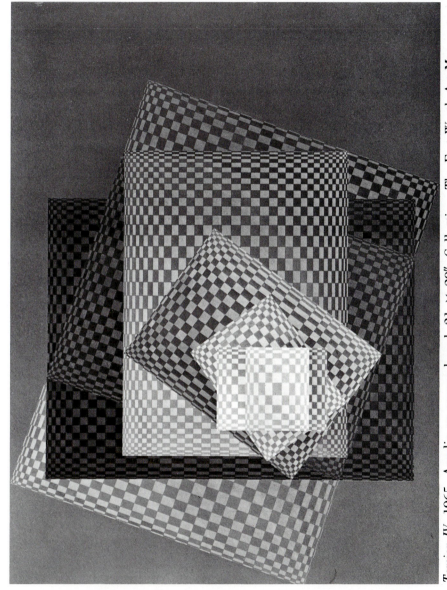

Torsion IV. 1965. Acrylic on canvas board, 21 × 28″. Collection, The Fort Worth Art Museum, Texas.

ELUSION, also done in 1950 (with a second version in 1952), is another attractive figure-ground work that manipulates film color to discover the effect of shadow on white. Because of the small, haloed form cradled within the larger ethereal shape, it was inevitable that this painting, created out of subtle films, would take on a madonna-and-child aspect for most viewers. Cunningham found that interpretation ironic as he was never interested in illustrating a figurative theme. He said, "The painting's meaning is, on a fundamental level, its visual content. There is no reason why a painting cannot have as its subject matter proportion, color, rhythm, or any other plastic elements. The objective of painting is to define a concept, not to illustrate it. The human nervous system is constant and we are continually trying to extend its language."[26]

Elusion II. 1950. Oil on canvas, 37½ × 28″. Private collection.

In his first major series of 1952, FIVE ASPECTS OF SCARLET, the artist was indeed immersed in his search to expand the visual language. The purpose of the series was to demonstrate that a color can look strikingly disparate depending on the colors surrounding it, since a different context yields a different experience.

In these works, rectangles are set in a pinwheel configuration, and at the center is a small rectangle of scarlet that remains constant in each painting. Although it never actually changes color, it appears differently in each work because of its relationship to the colors around it. It is also inhibited by the shadow or subtractive film over it, which, in illusion, removes the light. In these startling compositions, the implication is that if the film were lifted, a scarlet more luminous than any existing in nature would be revealed. This effect was what Cunningham thought to be one of his major achievements. He declared, "The thing I'm proudest of is the concept of color that can be seen in imagination outside of pigment limitations."[27] Then he went on to say, "If a painting tells us only what we already know (for example, that the sky is blue), there is no extension of our understanding. That extension is the purpose of art."[28]

In 1952, Cunningham painted DIFFRACTION III, a third version of a design he particularly liked. Diffraction is a modification light undergoes in passing by the edge of opaque bodies. Patsy Cunningham has commented that the definition does not quite fit and she has always felt the artist meant refraction which is a different phenomenon. Be that as it may, the painting does create the image of a moonscape with the light of the silvery, circular form being broken up into various planes. The work gives one the illusion of looking at the moon through a prism.

Ben and Patsy Cunningham, Yosemite, 1954. Photo: Michael Elsohn

In 1955, the Cunninghams bought a small Federal-period house on Carmine Street, in Greenwich Village. This was a fortuitous move after many years in a cramped apartment. The artist knocked out walls and redesigned the space for their own living quarters, doing all the cabinet work himself. More than half of the building was rented to bring in essential income. Until then, Cunningham's studios had been a succession of cheap, cold-water flats, which he often vacated one jump ahead of the wrecker's ball. He was now able to convert the attic into a spacious, skylighted studio.

Cunningham rebuilding Carmine Street interior, 1955

His first work in the big new studio was INVERTED INTERVALS, composed of graduated bands moving upward and outward in a progression of grays from light to dark. With its amorphous forms floating like projectiles in space, it has a kinship with the drawings and prints of Henry Moore and Barbara Hepworth. There is also a Surrealist element in the introduction of infinite space into the painting, but the sensitive concentration on close values from black to white is pure Cunningham.

40

Inverted Intervals. 1955. Oil on canvas, 48 × 60″. Collection, Morgan State University, Baltimore, Maryland.

By the late 1950s, Cunningham was in full stride, secure in his expressive medium. DEMATERIALIZATION, 1957, with its delicate forms suspended in space, is evidence of his mastery. The central shapes are based on the figure 8, and the intricacy of the film color is amazing. The artist, in a joking reference to the madonna-and-child image seen in his earlier ELUSION, suggested that the work be titled MOTHER AND CHILD IN A REVOLVING DOOR. However, the painting actually demonstrates the concept of dematerialized color which had preoccupied Cunningham for so many years. This work gives the illusion that the natural black content has been removed from the pigment and that there are films of light over the ground. The floating curvilinear forms look as though the artist had focused a soft illumination on his canvas and yet the light seems to be emanating from it.

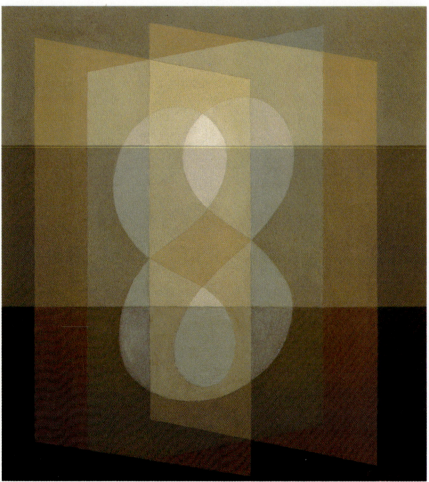

Dematerialization. 1957. Oil on canvas, 28 × 26″. Collection, Patsy Cunningham.

White Hidden and Revealed II. 1968.
Oil on canvas, 39 × 14″.

The callipygian forms appeared in Cunningham's work for the first time in 1958. Callipygian, a word of Greek origin, means literally beautiful buttocks, reminiscent of the shape of a woman's thigh as well as a Greek vase in the amphora form. Cunningham's use of it may have been an expression of his appreciation of the women in his life. The form first turns up in a painting called WHITE HIDDEN AND REVEALED in which he imposed two white films over a darker background. The artist achieved the illusion that if one of the films were peeled away, the viewer would discover a more brilliant white than any white imaginable. It was another attempt to imply a color that is more intense than anything available in pigment. Such was Cunningham's ingenuity that even though the gray of the ground and the gray of the film are identical, the illusion forces one to see the grays as distinctly different. A decade later he painted a second version in delicate, closer-valued grays.

LAOCOÖN, also done in 1958, is an example of how an external stimulus can motivate an artist. At this time Cunningham often waited at a particular bus stop in the evening hours. Across the street was a bar with a stainless steel front that reflected a neon light which the curving surface distorted. Cunningham's fascination with this visual image led to the painting LAOCOÖN, a work full of complex writhing motion, suggesting the Greek legend of Laocoön and his sons who were attacked by serpents coming from the sea. The painting has a blue ground covered by an elaborate network of films. Its twisting, contorted movement suggests a serpentine embrace from which one cannot escape.

Laocoön. 1958. Oil on canvas, 39 × 17″. Photo: Otto Nelson

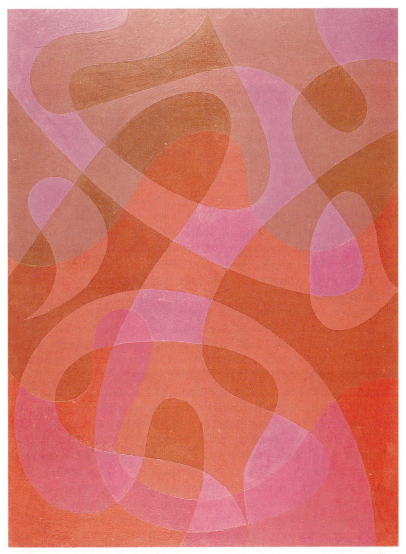

Ultraviolet Hallucination II. 1959. Oil on canvas board, 24 × 18″.
Collection, Clotildes Gleiberman, New York City.

As we have seen, Cunningham was continually attempting by the use
of illusionary films to suggest a color not accessible to the human eye.
He had always felt frustrated that he could not see ultraviolet or in-
frared. In his ULTRAVIOLET HALLUCINATION paintings, which he did
in two versions in 1959, the effect is that if the film were removed, one
would actually see the ultraviolet that is beyond the human eye's range.
In both works, he is using biomorphic imagery freely rather than the
more restrictive geometric shapes, but the forms are actually secondary
and his color dematerialization is the true subject of the work.

The year 1960 was a landmark in the painter's life. He felt the Newark School was becoming too conservative in its philosophy, so he resigned from the faculty and was invited, subsequently, to teach a design class at Cooper Union in New York. He was also invited to take part in two key exhibitions. One show at Cooper Union, called "The Logic and Magic of Color," included serious color work by Hiler and Albers. The other, "The Calculated Image" at the Morgan State College Art Gallery in Baltimore, was a bellwether exhibition. It acknowledged that directions in art, other than Abstract Expressionism, were worthy of exploration. Among the other artists shown were Joseph Albers, Jose de Rivera, Ellsworth Kelly, Kenneth Noland, Ludwig Sander, and Frank Stella.

At Cooper Union, as at Newark, Cunningham proved to be a dedicated and inspired teacher as well as a good friend to his students. Chris Wilmarth, the sculptor, who studied with him at this time wrote to him many years later saying, "The integrity of your teaching, the calm sureness of the room, really contributed to the quality of my life at that time. Ben, you and Patsy were really generous during some lonely moments."[29]

Cunningham's friend Reuben Kadish also testified as to the painter's loyalty and devotion to others. According to Kadish, Cunningham was extremely understanding, and in many cases was excessively generous with no thought of personal return. It was Cunningham who drew Kadish back into art after he had left it for some years.

It was also in 1960 that the artist finished a painting called the WATER SPRINKLER which he had worked on intermittently for many years. The subject of this painting came out of an experience he had had in 1946 while visiting a friend at Stony Brook, on Long Island. During that summer visit, Cunningham saw a water sprinkler at work and began making drawings of the utilitarian object. He was fascinated with the progression of films that the water was spinning out in a circle of parabolic shapes. For the next 14 years he kept coming back to this work, sometimes feeling he had finished it, but then feeling dissatisfied. Eventually, he knew he had captured the fragile and elusive image. Here, using a succession of films, he has taken a prosaic contraption and made a majestic image of it. It would remain one of his favorite paintings. In 1966, he produced a variation on this theme in the painting WATER SPRINKLER IN 2½ DIMENSIONS in which his almost flower-like forms maintain a tension between an intimation of space and the flat surface.

As noted, Cunningham was an artist who could work on a problem year after year without becoming bored with it, and he never concerned himself with the dictates of contemporary fashion in the art world. He had an aversion to easy answers and stated, "It's meaningless to do a painting when one knows how it will come out. Every painting should be a search for a revelation. I work by the illusion that I am not a picture maker, that I am an argonaut in the area of visual resolution."[30]

46

Water Sprinkler I. 1960. Oil on canvas, 27 × 54″. Collection, Sarah and William Lang, Southbury, Connecticut.

Water Sprinkler in 2½ Dimensions. 1966. Oil on canvas, 12¼ × 40¾″. Collection, Rodney and Sukey Wagner, Brooklyn, N.Y. Photo: Djordje Milićević.

48

In 1961, Cunningham did a more complicated version of the calli-pygian theme called SCULPTURED FILM using painted masonite as his medium. He cut out three small identical versions, models for a single large work over seven feet tall. SCULPTURED FILM, along with its coun-terparts, is a construction which the artist considered to be a drawing, with light and shadow creating the lines. This is a bas-relief, composed of cut-out forms, but the brilliant use of light and shadow produces the illusion of subtle overlays of films of varying tones. There is also a sense of high energy from the suggestion of rapid movement created by the elegant films. Later, in 1967, the painter would visit Greece where his devotion to classical Greek design as demonstrated by these callipygian forms would be intensely reaffirmed.

Sculptured Film. 1965. Oil on masonite, 7' 8½" × 5'. Collection, Tweed Museum of Art, University of Minnesota-Duluth.

49

Callipygia I. 1962. Oil on tapestry canvas, 7' 8½" × 5'. Collection, Tweed Museum of Art, University of Minnesota-Duluth.

Also during 1961, the Cunninghams traveled throughout the British Isles and then returned to Paris for several weeks. During that period they visited a number of churches with magnificent stained-glass windows. MODULUS, a large painting in rectilinear images on four panels within a single frame, was done in 1962. This work, which could serve as a religious icon, convinces the viewer that he is seeing glowing light filtered through stained glass.

CALLIPYGIA I, 1962, already mirrored in the constructions of 1961, is the first large painted version of the callipygian theme. In color it echoes the dematerialized purples of the earlier ULTRAVIOLET paintings, and its shapes are anthropomorphic. Drawn to the essential human form, the artist was always seeking new ways to express it.

50

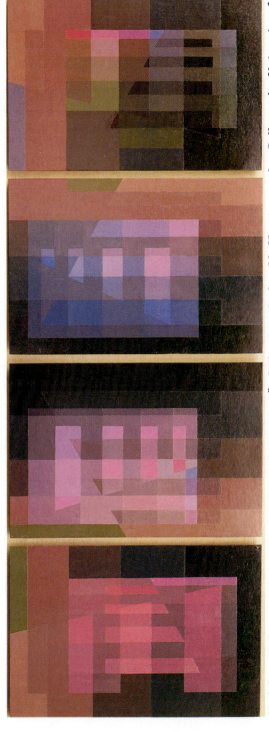

Modulus. 1962. Oil on 4 canvas panels, each 36 × 24″. Collection, Archer M. Huntington Art Gallery, the University of Texas at Austin, Michener Art Fund, 1969.

In 1963, Cunningham had his first one-man show in New York at the Castellane Gallery on Madison Avenue. He called the exhibition "Telesis," which is defined as the attainment of desired ends by the application of intelligent human effort to the means. Later he would amplify the definition in a statement of his own philosophy: "The means pay homage to the miracle of vision. The end is to honor the spirit of man."[31] With this title, the painter proclaimed to an art world steeped in the automatism of action painting and dedicated to the ideal of keeping any control or plan out of the work, that his art was indeed controlled and planned. It was a strong statement announcing his independence. The exhibition was favorably reviewed in *The New York Times* and sold well, but in the New York art world, just emerging from Abstract Expressionist domination and reacting to the shock of Pop Art, it made only a small ripple.

Cunningham kept on with his work and completed RED REREAD that year. It was his first tondo and an early use of the motif of the folding form he would utilize in many paintings to come. As in many of his works, the title provides the clue as to what is happening in the work itself. In this painting, the films that function against a brilliant green background can be seen as either red or green but they are in actuality gray. Cunningham could have been thinking of this tour-de-force work when he wrote:

> *In nearly all cases, a new language is essential to a fresh contribution. The science of color is a new visual language for our time just as the discovery of perspective as a symbol for three-dimensional space was for Renaissance artists. A painter cannot be a colorist without knowing that burnt sienna is orange with black in it and knowing how it relates to other pigments which have more or less black content. Accurate verbal terminology is missing in color—and what I mean is layers of relationship, not merely verbal terms. Two tubes labeled red and green do not express the same thing as "polar attributes of the same sensation."[32]*

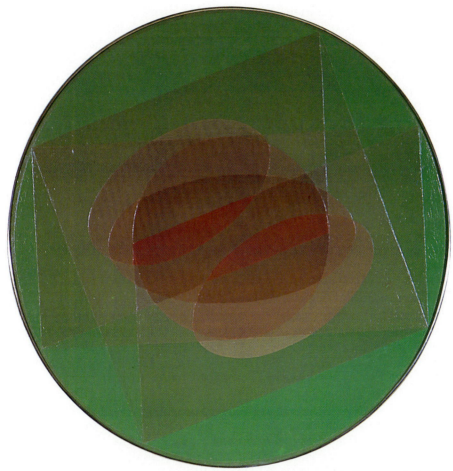

Red Reread. 1963. Oil on canvas board, 31″ diameter. Collection, Robert and Carol Straus, Houston, Texas.

In 1964, Bruno Palmer-Poroner of the East Hampton Gallery in New York City contacted Cunningham because there were intimations that something called "Optical Art" was about to dominate the New York art scene and he had heard that Cunningham was a practitioner of it. The artist was mystified by the label but pleased when the dealer offered him a one-man exhibition. He was doubly pleased when the curator William Seitz chose his painting EQUIVOCATION for inclusion in "The Responsive Eye" exhibition to be held early in 1965 at the Museum of Modern Art. Thus, through the advent of what was soon to be known as Op Art, the New York art world was finally catching up to Ben Cunningham.

EQUIVOCATION, done in 1964, was one of the most frequently reproduced paintings in the highly acclaimed exhibition and certainly one of the stars of the show. Cunningham produced eight other such works during this period using a type of orthographic projection (in which the projecting lines are perpendicular to the plane of projection) to achieve the illusion of three-dimensional form in two-dimensional space. According to the painter, the series grew out of a problem he devised for his class at Cooper Union to sharpen their visual perception. The availability of acrylic paints was another factor. EQUIVOCATION, set in a yellow color volume, took 100 steps to graduate from the lightest to the darkest color. Note that the color in the tessera pattern in the upper left corner, which appears so dark, is the same as the light color in the lower right. Had the painting been done in slow-drying oils, it would have taken a very long time to complete the adjustments necessary to achieve the color progression. Because of its fast-drying property, acrylic was found to be a much easier medium with which to work. Later he became bored with it because it ceased to be a challenge—a typical Cunningham response—and went back to oils.

EQUIVOCATION was a painting of special significance to the artist. He said, "For me the work has a time-binding quality in terms of my development as a painter. It applies a new technology to an earlier visual symbol system (contained or conjoined shadow, perhaps more familiarly known as chiaroscuro) which I originally explored in my NUDE WITH PINK RIBBON of 1931 and DESERT of 1939, yet it achieves its own identity in the process."[33]

Charlotte Willard of the *New York Post* wrote of EQUIVOCATION that its "small squares form funnels, large squares and cones which drop, turn, and twist as you watch it, like a cinema background from the 'Cabinet of Dr. Caligari.' "[34]

Some have observed that in its use of certain formal devices, EQUIVOCATION is similar to the work of the artist Victor Vasarely. It should be noted, however, that Cunningham had not been familiar with Vaserely's paintings and it was coincidental that he and Vasarely developed interests in similar problems in painting at the same time. Their paths crossed during this particular period but took quite different directions before and after this short interlude.

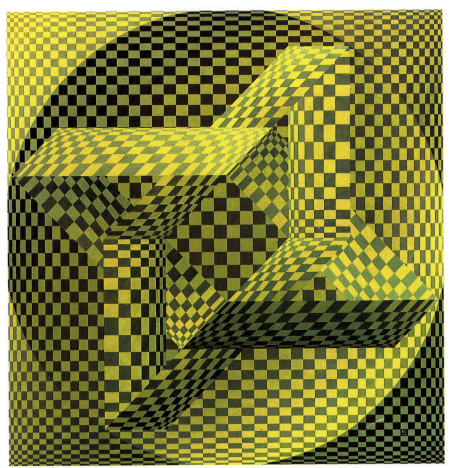

Equivocation. 1964. Synthetic polymer paint on composition board, 26 × 26″ (65.9 × 65.9 cm). Collection, The Museum of Modern Art, New York. Larry Aldrich Foundation Fund. 106.65.

On the basis of this one extraordinarily intricate painting, the artist received a considerable amount of attention from the art and mass media. He was discussed in art journals and dailies, interviewed by Mike Wallace on television and by John Daly on radio. He was labeled the father, or even more reverentially, the grandfather of Op Art. Cunningham, however, was never comfortable with those labels as he thought them conceptually meaningless and agreed with Joseph Albers's comment that the term Optical Art was as tautological as "navigational sailing" or "ambulatory walking." In any case, Cunningham's work was much more complicated than most of the paintings in "The Responsive Eye" exhibition. As Robert Zakanitch puts it, "His works were so complex but he came in at a time when everyone was doing simplistics. They didn't know how to look at it or get the significance of what was going on."[35]

At the same time, a great deal of controversy surrounded the major Museum of Modern Art exhibition. Critics thought some of the work simpleminded—just candy for the eyes—which had nothing to do with man's deeper emotional, intellectual, or philosophical responses. Cunningham was sometimes associated with these practitioners of optical exercises because his work was exhibited along with theirs. This was an unfortunate irony for an artist who had defined the goal of a painter as the exploration of ideas rather than the exploitation of effects.

On the other hand, there were critics who understood the full implications of Cunningham's work. Michael Lenson, familiar with Cunningham's paintings before the museum show, wrote of him in the *Newark Sunday News:*

> *Though a creator of optical illusions, he was always more sensitively restrained and less mechanical than most of his own or the movement's satellites. Thus it is not by accident that Cunningham's EQUIVOCATION is one of the real fascinations of the Museum show. Rather than call it "Op" we'll call it what it is—extraordinary painting.*[36]

Writing in 1966, Lawrence Campbell also rejected the Op label, saying, " 'Op' is a term too limiting and undignified to apply to the magnitude of Cunningham's achievements."[37]

Later, in 1969, Campbell wrote:

> *His passion for color theory—dating from the 1930s— makes him a pioneer in the development which in the middle 1960s abruptly crystallized as "Op." But, unlike most Op artists, Cunningham plays on the entire scale of perceptual themes: simultaneous contrasts of colors; after-images; depth illusions induced by color rather than by linear perspective; color as temperature. . . . .*[38]

Fully understood or not, the attention focused on EQUIVOCATION at the time of the MOMA show gave a great impetus to Cunningham's career. His paintings were acquired by major museums and collectors, and he was invited to participate in many significant exhibitions. In 1965, at the age of 61, for the first time in his life, his paintings began to support him financially.

During the same year in which he completed EQUIVOCATION, the artist painted EMERGING EMERAUDE, which led to other works with similar motifs. EMERGING EMERAUDE, with its concave and convex forms in a red volume, has an area of gray illusory film which, as one looks through it, becomes a vivid, magical green. As in EQUIVOCATION, ambiguous perspectives tease the eye. One can see the folding forms as the bottom of an image looked up through, or the top of an image looked down into. SQUARE ROOT OF MINUS NINE again combines the folding forms with the convex and concave.

Emerging Emeraude. 1964. Acrylic on canvas board, 24 × 24″.
Collection, Maria and Henry Feiwel, New York City.

Square Root of Minus Nine. 1965. Acrylic on canvas board, 16 × 48″. Collection, Harcourt Brace Jovanovich, Inc.

Painting for the Night-Adapted Eye. 1964. Acrylic on canvas board, 28 × 36″. Private collection.

Among the other acrylic paintings of this period, PAINTING FOR THE NIGHT-ADAPTED EYE, in a grid format, beautifully demonstrates night vision, when we see blue with great intensity. During the day our eye is more red-sensitive.

In INDUCTIVE HALATION, 1965, the artist concentrated on a different problem, painting in close values in order to induce or create the illusion of light or halation at the bottom of each band of color.

Over the years, many had suggested that the artist do another corner painting large enough to give one the sense of being able to walk into it. Going back to oil paints, his primary love, Cunningham, late in 1965, executed a large work (over six feet tall), using almost the same basic design as the original CORNER PAINTING. In this work, however, he did not move into yellow or red as in the original, but kept it within a close and subtle monochromatic range. SIX DIMENSIONS OF ORANGE deals with the color orange in terms of temperature (warm and cold), valence (strong and weak), and value (light and dark). This painting takes a corner and makes a glowing orange world of it. Like its predecessor, it is composed of two sections that meet at the right angle of the walls, and through the magic of color contrasts and wise placement of geometric forms, gives the illusion of penetrating the intersection by moving perspectively back into space. The work produces in the viewer the sensation of actually moving into a fairy-tale room filled with magic mirrors.

This phenomenal work was exhibited in the Whitney Annual and widely acclaimed. John Canaday of *The New York Times*, in awarding imaginary prizes to the ten most outstanding works in the show, proclaimed: "To Ben Cunningham of New York, a prize yet to be named for SIX DIMENSIONS OF ORANGE, a play with multiple perspectives, expertly constructed."[39] Emily Genauer, another highly respected critic, reacting to Cunningham's painting and another work by Richard Anuszkiewicz, called both artists "consummate craftsmen with intensely personal insights." She went on to say, "They take their place in this survey, not as exponents of a limited point of view, but as immensely gifted artists utilizing a specific direction to reach their own expressive goals."[40]

Cunningham working on *Six Dimensions of Orange*, 1965. Photo: Hannes Beckmann

Six Dimensions of Orange. 1965. Oil on canvas, 2 sections, 81 × 114″, 81 × 57″.

61

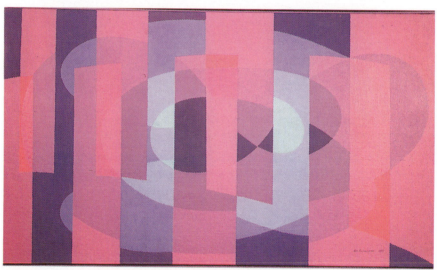

Counter Themes, Resolved. 1966. Oil on canvas, 28 × 50″. Collection, Joan and George Wallace, New York City.

Further evidence of Cunningham's return to oil is demonstrated in a series of three paintings called COUNTER THEMES, executed in 1965–66. As companion pieces, he did three constructions of identical size and similar motif called THEMES. In a design called THEME a in one construction, and a design called THEME 1 in another, it was not accidental that he used a curvilinear letter *a* and a rectilinear number *1* to describe, respectively, a curvilinear and a rectilinear construction. Then he composed THEMES 1b which wittily combined the rectilinear and the curvilinear shapes, superimposing the curvilinear over the rectilinear. In the COUNTER THEMES paintings, using a sophisticated play of film color, he took the same forms and put them into three different color relationships.

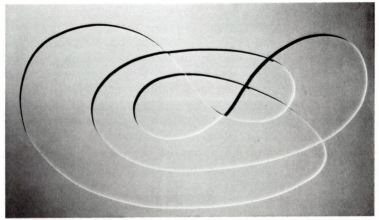

Theme a. 1966. Painted styrofoam and casein, 28 × 50″.

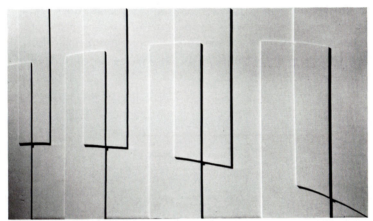

Theme 1. 1966. Painted styrofoam and casein, 28 × 50″.
Collection, Patsy Cunningham.

Themes 1b. 1966. Painted styrofoam and casein, 28 × 50″.
Collection, Mr. and Mrs. John F. Lott, Lubbock, Texas.

Occasionally, during the years to come, the artist would return to acrylic for its fast-drying property when working with extremely close color runs. Basically, however, he preferred the organic "skin" of an oil painting to the synthetic and relatively lifeless texture of acrylic.

The late '60s were among the most fulfilling and productive years of Cunningham's life. Income from his paintings enabled him to lighten his teaching schedule considerably. Now his struggle was to resist the demands made upon him as the designated originator of Op Art and to keep strictly to his own vision. Cunningham, always a loner, was wise enough to realize that "before recognition an artist tries to avoid labels. After recognition he tries to destroy the labels applied to his work."[41] He also commented:

> *The painters one admires are the ones who try, perhaps unsuccessfully, to do better than they have done. Those who destroy your illusions are the ones who run to the marketplace again and again with what they have already done or who do less than their potential. So that an "unsuccessful" painting may be more rewarding than a "successful" one.*[42]

Cunningham at the Cooper Union, 1965. Photo: Monroe Litman.

64

Cunningham at the Cooper Union, 1965. Photo: Monroe Litman.

Predictably, Cunningham did not rest on his laurels. Always out to extend the visual language, he went on to execute HYPERCUBE STUDY, in 1966, which anticipates his involvement with the tesseract. A tessera is one of the small tiles used in mosaic work. If its square face is projected, it becomes a tesseract, or a cube in four dimensions. The fourth dimension is time. Cunningham's involvement in the tesseract theme reflected his intense emotional response to works in mosaic, particularly those of the Church of San Vitale in Ravenna and of the Karyë Museum in Istanbul.

The HYPERCUBE STUDY creates a mandala-like image in which cubes emerge and can be seen by the viewer in varied formats over a prolonged time period. Resembling a stylized flower form, the painting, called a study but actually a finished work, is an amazing visualization of the concept of time passing. During a close examination, one can see 16 cubes forming and reforming in various combinations.

Cunningham became deeply involved in the tesseract theme and did a number of paintings and constructions based on the motif. His painting called TESSERACT, which followed the HYPERCUBE STUDY in 1966, successfully replaced a version done ten years before. The earlier painting had never completely satisfied the artist. He ultimately destroyed it.

In TACTILE TESSERACT, 1967, the hypercube image appears again in a different medium, a large corner construction done with painted masonite. Through the use of line and shadow, the piece, though painted in off-white, manifests a varied value range. CHROMATIC TESSERACT, 1968, done in oil on two panels, is another miracle of complexity with brilliant cubes emerging as the viewer studies it. In contrast, a painting of the same year, ACHROMATIC TESSERACT, is limited to the simple values of black, white, and gray.

Hypercube Study. 1966. Oil on canvas, 24″ diameter. Collection, Julie B. Isenberg, Memphis, Tennessee. Photo: Otto Nelson.

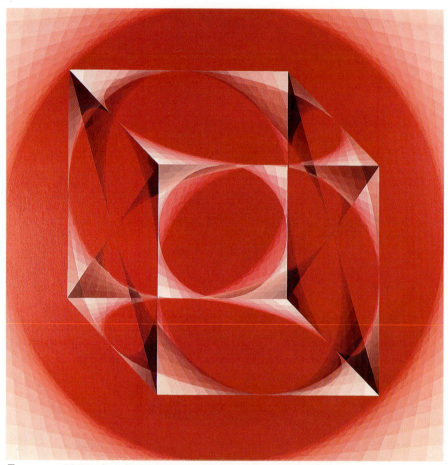

Tesseract. 1966. Acrylic on canvas board, 30 × 30″. Collection, Mrs. John D. Murchison, Dallas, Texas.

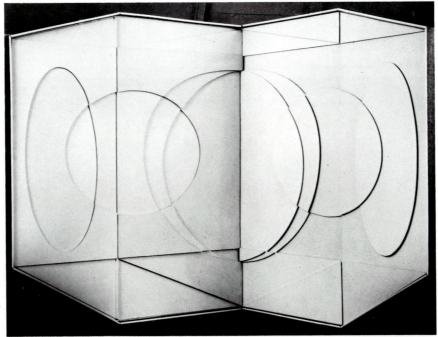

Tactile Tesseract. 1967. Painted masonite, 2 sections, 47 × 44″ each.
Photo: Otto Nelson.

Achromatic Tesseract. 1968. Oil on canvas, 32 × 54″. Private collection.
Photo: Otto Nelson.

Turanian Turquoise. 1966. Oil on canvas, 28 × 46″.

In 1966, a trip to Turkey inspired two paintings of that year. Turquoise is, of course, the French word for Turkish, and the artist paid homage to the brilliant color encountered everywhere in the tiles and mosques of Istanbul. In NOCTURNAL TURQUOISE the turquoise moves out of the dark, brownish background, while in TURANIAN TURQUOISE, the colors are reversed with the brown emerging from the intense turquoise background. Both works are a stately progression of organic and geometric forms built out of films that appear to move backward and forward in space. Certainly there is an element of poetry in these images, although Cunningham questioned the word as a descriptive term in dealing with painting. He insisted, "For this painter, the key word is 'visual.' To say that a painting is 'poetic' makes as little sense to me as calling an architectural structure 'terpsichorean.' I would suggest that what all art forms do have in common and what gives them an enduring quality is an underlying order and structure—the projected structure and order of the human nervous system itself."[43]

70

During one of his visits to London, Cunningham had found a wax medium with an accommodating texture and he used it instead of oil as the vehicle for his painting SPRING SUMMATION of 1967. In this work he combined two forms to make a third, as he had done in earlier "summation" themes. Cubes interplay with folding forms and are combined with color presented as additive films to increase the intensity of the light. The painting culminates in a central rectangle that blazes forth as if a spotlight were focused on it.

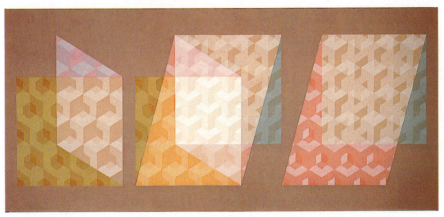

Spring Summation. 1967. Wax on canvas panel, 26 × 58″.

The following year was a time of change. In 1968, Cunningham left Cooper Union and assumed a painting instructorship at the venerable Art Students League of New York. The school suited his temperament ideally since it used the atelier method and teachers were free of administrative interference. All classes were elective, and his soon attracted a large enrollment.

Cunningham at the Art Students League, 1971.

Elegy. 1968. Oil on canvas, 28 × 46″. Collection, Dr. Clarice J. Kestenbaum, New York City.

It was also a time of mourning. Three close friends of the artist had recently died, among them his beloved French friend, Albert Rémy, and his comrade in color, Hilaire Hiler. Cunningham felt the losses keenly and in 1968 painted ELEGY. In this work, composed of surface and volume color, there is a Surrealist sense of space in which gray stretches into blue into infinity. Three majestic oval forms, perhaps symbolizing the three departed friends, seem to express both containment and depletion. The painter was having his first glimpse into the void which he would explore with even more intensity later on.

During the same year, Cunningham reached back in time to take inspiration from an experience he had had at the Pitti Palace in Florence in 1949. He had seen a magnificently ornamented Renaissance chest there and had questioned the guard as to its purpose. He was told it was the jewel case of one of the Medici women. Overwhelmed by the ornate container, the artist exclaimed to his wife, "What kind of jewels could you put in a case like that?"

His painting JEWELS OF THE MEDICI was the answer. This work is composed of three panels that form a trapezoid and create the illusion of two open-faced cubes divided by a single wall. The brilliantly patterned case, formed by the cubes, glows with an unearthly blue-green light. According to Patsy Cunningham, the beautiful, complicated container evolved very quickly. The artist used color in its most sophisticated form, as it is seen with cone vision where "temperature must be adjusted and then the critical area becomes valence: strength; brightness; saturation of hue."[44] Indeed, the jewel box is a wondrously intricate image, with its interconnected transparent planes of color. But the jewels themselves were very difficult for the painter to articulate. Ultimately, he painted them achromatically, using the value contrasts and three-dimensional images associated with rod vision. According to Cunningham, "Cone vision adds to basic seeing the dividend of color, a gift from the gods. Rod vision is what we survive with. It is the common sensor which distinguishes form and lets us differentiate between light and dark."[45] As it turned out, only this less elaborate vision would create the jewels successfully in the context of the painting. Indeed, the astral-shaped form encased in its pale crystalline sphere is the very center of this mandala image. Buried in the stuff of everyday vision is the essence of the human mystery, the beauty of creation, the beginning of the journey into the spiritual.

A visitor to the A. M. Sachs gallery, where JEWELS OF THE MEDICI was first shown, was moved to write to the artist: "A person does not ordinarily perceive images like this at any length in his daily existence. There's such a rich well of profound stimulus that people need to look at this painting many times for long periods before even beginning to absorb the fullest measure of its enormous content."[46]

Jewels of the Medici. 1968. Oil on 3 canvas panels for installation on a projecting corner, 4 × 8' left wall, 3 × 3' right wall.

In 1969, the artist returned to the tesseract theme in one of his rare prints, a corner work entitled SCARLET TESSERACT. During the year, the color scarlet dominated other works as well, among them, two series of four paintings, respectively known as SCARLET MODULATIONS and SCARLET CONTINUUM. All these works are variations on a theme and resemble the tesseract in that one can see forms continually surfacing, disappearing, and redefining themselves into different geometric shapes. Cunningham's frequent use of scarlet, when working in New York, may have been due to reflected light in his studio from the red brick buildings across the street, just as his Paris paintings often reflected the blue-violet light of that city. These intense responses are not surprising given the artist's sensitivity to color. Cunningham, aware of these environmental influences, made use of them not to paint a naturalistic scene but to explore the properties of the hue in question. This approach was typical of him and he said, "The stimulus is out there. The important thing is to *use* it not illustrate it."[47]

At this time the painter continued at peak performance, applying the sum of his experience not only to new themes but to subjects he had explored in the past. Thus the two scarlet series relate to his earlier FIVE ASPECTS OF SCARLET and a series called FOUR VIEWS OF VERMILION, done in 1963. In the SCARLET CONTINUUM paintings, scarlet is the constant as in the earlier works. The central rectangle is always the same hue but functions so diversely that it seems to be a different color in each work. There is a musical analogy in these paintings, and the continuum can be likened to a harpischord or bass that holds the structure together while the other instruments embroider on the theme.

Scarlet Tesseract. 1969. Silk screen on polystyrol, 2 panels, 30 × 30″ each, edition of 125.

Scarlet Modulation I. 1969. Oil on canvas board, 18 × 24″. Collection, Mr. and Mrs. John F. Lott, Lubbock, Texas.

Scarlet Continuum II. 1969. Oil on canvas board, 18 × 24″. Private collection.

Another work of 1969 represented a return to and an extension beyond the past. In 1963 the artist had done a painting called AUTUMN NONSCAPE, a large work that came back damaged from an exhibition. He never forgot the painting but did not want to make a replica of it, so he took its basic forms but gave it colors associated with spring. The older work was reborn with the title of JEUNE JAUNE (Young Yellow), a reference to the color of leaves when they first appear before they become deep green. In this painting, which is a combination of rectangular and curvilinear forms, a series of subtle films against a dark ground carry the eye from an intense yellow to the ultimate leaf green. It is an essential rather than a literal depiction of spring. Once again, Cunningham is exploring the structure behind the appearance of things, the true nature of reality.

Cunningham with work in progress, *Jeune Jaune*, Carmine Street studio, 1969. Photo: Budd.

78

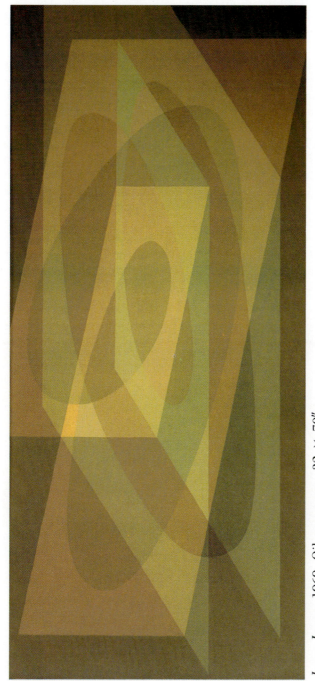

Jeune Jaune. 1969. Oil on canvas, 32 × 70″.

While 1969 proved to be a highly productive year in the studio, it was also the year that the artist's health began to fail. The problem took the form of a slow deterioration that affected his mental outlook and personality as well as his physical well-being. Normally a man of warm and relaxed disposition, Cunningham now became increasingly withdrawn, anxious, and depressed. His wife worried more and more, and doctors offered few answers and little advice.

In the summer of 1970, thinking that a change of scene might be salutary, the Cunninghams rented the top floor of a house in the little village of Lyme Center, New Hampshire. There, the artist seemed to work out his physical and emotional problems in a painting called GORDIAN KNOT. This work in acrylic, begun in New York, presents a monochromatic run in red which is in a red field as well. Certainly its twisting, entangled motif is expressive of the painter's state of mind at this period. According to his wife, he was "tied in knots" due to the undefined problems that were assailing him. But despite the stressful circumstances he was as meticulous as ever, and before he executed GORDIAN KNOT he organized a color structure in which a particularly beautiful progression gives the illusion of creating bands of light as in the earlier work INDUCTIVE HALATION.

Gordian Knot. 1970. Acrylic on canvas panel, 25 × 30″.

80

Threshold of Space. 1970. Acrylic on canvas, 20 × 30″. Collection, Mr. and Mrs. K. W. Kirkpatrick, Post, Texas.

That summer also saw Cunningham's last acrylic painting, THRESHOLD OF SPACE, which was closely related to the earlier ELEGY. But if that work was a reaction to the death of friends, THRESHOLD OF SPACE may be seen as a visual attempt to come to terms with death in general and possibly his own in particular. In this small but amazingly powerful work, the painter has filled his space with an ambiance of cool, blue light and then, with the grays and whites of perspectively formed squares, has drawn our vision back into the nothingness of the opaque blue beyond. Yet even as we advance into the unknown, amorphous cut-out rectangles block our seemingly inevitable journey over the edge of infinity. We must accept, as the artist accepts, that the mystery is not to be penetrated. As Cunningham once said, "Painting is a spiritual activity which is an investigation of unknown areas."[48]

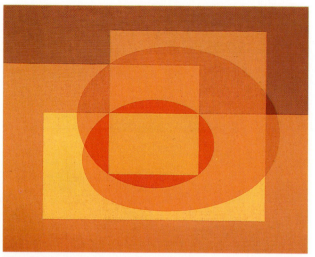

Threshold of Orange. 1970. Oil on canvas board, 22 × 30″. Collection, Mr. and Mrs. John F. Lott, Lubbock, Texas.

A series of paintings, also done in New Hampshire, puts the word "threshold" into a different context. Each of these six works in oil presents a major hue (THRESHOLD OF RED, THRESHOLD OF YELLOW, etc.). In each painting, however, the color is inhibited by an illusory shadow so that the eye remains on the threshold, never experiencing the pure hue. It is something of a visual tease. The series demonstrates Cunningham's idea that " 'feeling' in a painting could be enhanced (controlled? attained?) very often by working below the threshold of perception."[49]

Threshold of Yellow. 1970. Oil on canvas board, 22 × 30″.

Refreshed by the New Hampshire summer, Cunningham returned to New York to produce PASCAL PROJECTION, a joyous work. Here he used film color brilliantly to create luminous circles of different colors at the points where basic oval forms overlap.

Pascal Projection. 1970. Oil on canvas, 34 × 28″. Collection, Rosalie Berkowitz, New York City.

During 1971, Cunningham's health continued to fail. In an attempt to restore his depressed spirits, his wife suggested a return to Nevada. So for four months in the late summer and fall of that year, the couple rented a small house in the foothills above Reno. It was the terrain Cunningham loved, and they spent much time with his old friend Arthur Lyon, who took them by car on trips throughout the state. Out of these excursions, the painter produced a series of three, small, lovely paintings called NEVADA I, II, and III. In these compositions, he presents different treatments of the same basic theme, juxtaposing geometrical and organic films to achieve an incredibly intense turquoise that emerges from the earthier desert colors. It is uncanny—as if Cunningham had returned to his beloved Pyramid Lake after 30 years and had portrayed it, at last, in a vision that was uniquely his own.

The NEVADA series would be Cunningham's final tribute to the desert country of his youth. After his return to New York, he continued to work and teach, struggling against ill health. Then, one day in June, 1972, he fell and suffered brain damage. It is a testament to his gallant spirit that, during the next year, he undertook a large new version of the callipygian theme. Sadly, however, he was not able to complete it in a manner commensurate with his highest standards.

On April 5, 1975, the artist died.

Nevada III. 1971. Oil on canvas board, 22 × 28″. Collection, Mr. and Mrs. John F. Lott, Lubbock, Texas.

At one point in his career, Cunningham had told John Daly in an interview, "Someone once said that a contribution occurs when a sensitive person meets a new language. We now have what might be called an exact science, or relatively exact science—color. So this becomes a new language. A man with imagination can now use color as a tool to communicate. I would like to be the one who makes that contribution."[50]

Since his death, Cunningham's work has been included in several exhibitions, not the least of which was an impressive show of his corner paintings at the Neuberger Museum at Purchase, New York. There has yet to be, however, widespread acknowledgement of Ben Cunningham's massive contribution to the history of modern art in the area of color. Possibly no other artist has gained such an astonishing mastery over its intricacies, and few artists, in our time, have extended its subtle, visual possibilities to the degree that this painter has done with such depths of feeling.

Time, as we have seen, was an important dimension in Cunningham's work. In another sense, time was a major element in his philosophy. "Time-binding" was the term he used to describe his profession, which he saw as a continuing bridge between generations and cultures. While it is difficult to predict any artist's place in art history, a continuing process of review and revision, surely it is not premature to say that time is on the side of Ben Cunningham.

WORKS ILLUSTRATED   PAGE

FOOTNOTES

[1]Lawrence Campbell, "The Well-Tempered Color-Wheel," *Art News*, 68. No. 2 (April, 1969), 42.

[2]Edited transcript interview, Ben Cunningham in "New York, New York," with John Daly, Voice of America, (Radio) USIA Broadcast, November 25, 1970, 8.

[3]Patsy Cunningham in discussion with Cindy Nemser, November 20, 1984.

[4]Ben Cunningham. Recollections. Catalog, WPA Artists Then and Now, Inaugural exhibition, YM-YWHA of Essex Co., N.J., October, 1967.

[5]Hilaire Hiler, "A Painter Tries to Articulate," *Contact*, 1, No. 3 (October, 1932), 12.

[6]Vincent Schmidt, "The Structuralism of Hilaire Hiler and Its Relationship to Other Tendencies in Art, "Hilaire Hiler and Structuralism: New Conception of Form-Color, ed. Waldemar George, texts by Hilaire Hiler and Vincent Schmidt, trans. by Edouard Rodit, and Anna Elsabeth Leroy. (New York: George Wittenborn Inc., 1958), 21.

[7]Hilaire Hiler, "The Artist and Scientific Method," A paper prepared for the American Artists' Professional League, (February 24, 1945), 7.

[8]*Ibid*.

[9]Ben Cunningham, Statement, November 8, 1964.

[10]Letter from Ben Cunningham to Faber Birren, January 22, 1968.

[11]Ben Cunningham, Notes taken by Patsy Cunningham, Duluth, Minnesota, August 8, 1967.

[12]Ben Cunningham, Notes taken by Patsy Cunningham, New York, New York, December 24, 1968.

[13]Ben Cunningham Catalog, Retrospective, Tweed Museum, University of Minnesota, Duluth, (May 4–21, 1967).

[14]David Katz, *World of Color*, cited in Lawrence Campbell, "The Well-Tempered Color-Wheel," *Art News, op cit.*, 70.

[15]Interview with Reuben Kadish by Cindy Nemser, February 27, 1985.

[16]Interview with Robert Zakanitch by Cindy Nemser, March 5, 1985.

[17]Letter to Patsy Cunningham from Frank Gauna, artist and former student, October, 1974.

[18]Faber Birren, *History of Color in Painting*, (New York, Reinhold, 1965), 138.

[19]Letter to Ben Cunningham from artist Jean Varda, September, 1952.

[20]Ben Cunningham, Statement to East Hampton Gallery, New York, February 9, 1965.

[21]Obituary, *Art Students' League News*, 28, No. 4 (April, 1975), 1.

[22]Robert Zakanitch, *op. cit.*

[23]Ben Cunningham, Notes taken by Patsy Cunningham, New York, New York, March 23, 1969.

[24]Ben Cunningham, Notes taken by Patsy Cunningham, New York, New York, May 20, 1969.

CAL
ND
237
C8496
N46
1989

In Memory Of

Patricia Griffin Cunningham

While form is absolute, so that you can say at the moment you draw any line that it is either right or wrong, color is wholly relative. Every hue throughout your work is altered by every touch that you add in other places; so that what was warm a minute ago, becomes cold when you have put a hotter color in another place, and what was in harmony when you left it, becomes discordant as you set other colors beside it; so that every touch must be laid, not with a view to its effect at the time, but with a view to its effect in futurity, the result upon it of all that is afterwards to be done being previously considered. You may easily understand that, this being so, nothing but the devotion of life, and great genius besides, can make a colorist . . . To color perfectly is the rarest and most precious power an artist can possess.

John Ruskin, *Modern Painters*

[25]Ajay, Abe. Monograph on Ben Cunningham for *Corner Paintings* exhibition, Neuberger Museum, Purchase, N.Y., October, 1975.

[26]Ben Cunningham, Notes taken by Patsy Cunningham, New York, New York, June 18, 1968.

[27]Ben Cunningham, Notes taken by Patsy Cunningham, New York, New York, November 11, 1967.

[28]Ben Cunningham statement in response to request from Project Outreach, Detroit Institute of Arts, December 8, 1968.

[29]Letter to Ben Cunningham from Chris Wilmarth, artist and former student, February 1972.

[30]Ben Cunningham, Notes taken by Patsy Cunningham, New York, New York, May 22, 1968.

[31]Notes written by Ben Cunningham on route to Baltimore by train, November 1, 1968.

[32]Ben Cunningham, Notes taken by Patsy Cunningham, New York, New York, August 8, 1967.

[33]Ben Cunningham, Statement for Museum of Modern Art for their records on artists in the collections, April 10, 1969.

[34]Charlotte Willard, "Review of Responsive Eye," *New York Post*, (February 20, 1965), 46.

[35]Robert Zakanitch, *op. cit.*

[36]Michael Lenson, "Review of MOMA 'Responsive Eye,' " *Newark Sunday News*, (March 7, 1965), Sect. I.

[37]Lawrence Campbell, essay accompanying the publication of *Hypothetical Hypercube*, commissioned by Springbok Editions, 1966.

[38]Lawrence Campbell, "The Well-Tempered Color-Wheel," *Art News*, 68, No. 2, (April, 1969), 42–43.

[39]John Canaday, "Whitney Annual," *New York Times*, December 8, 1965.

[40]Emily Genauer, "The Facts Up to Date at the Whitney Annual," *New York Herald Tribune*, December 12, 1965.

[41]Ben Cunningham, Notes taken by Patsy Cunningham, New York, New York, November 12, 1967.

[42]Ben Cunningham, Notes taken by Patsy Cunningham, New York, New York, September 28, 1968.

[43]Ben Cunningham, Statement, November 8, 1964.

[44]Ben Cunningham, Notes taken by Patsy Cunningham, New York, New York, Autumn, 1966.

[45]Ben Cunningham, Discussion with Cindy Nemser, July, 1973.

[46]Letter to Ben Cunningham from Bernard Curtin, April, 1969.

[47]Ben Cunningham, Statement in response to request from Project Outreach, *op. cit.*

[48]Ben Cunningham, Notes taken by Patsy Cunningham, New York, New York, January 11, 1968.

[49]Ben Cunningham, Notes taken by Patsy Cunningham, New York, New York, April 18, 1967.

[50]Edited transcript interview, Ben Cunningham in "New York, New York," with John Daly, Voice of America (Radio) USIA, Broadcast, November 25, 1970, 1–2.